The Iran Hostage Crisis: The History of the Sta
Contacts Between the United Sta

By Charles River Editors

A picture of Iranian students storming the U.S. embassy in Tehran

About Charles River Editors

Charles River Editors provides superior editing and original writing services across the digital publishing industry, with the expertise to create digital content for publishers across a vast range of subject matter. In addition to providing original digital content for third party publishers, we also republish civilization's greatest literary works, bringing them to new generations of readers via ebooks.

Sign up here to receive updates about free books as we publish them, and visit Our Kindle Author Page to browse today's free promotions and our most recently published Kindle titles.

Introduction

A picture of two of the hostages behind held at the embassy

The Iran Hostage Crisis

"Carter's predecessor, whom he says he emulates -- Harry Truman -- would have landed the Marines and offered to cripple Iran's economic base. These Iranians have committed an act of war against the United States and all Carter wants to do at the moment is talk. It is time to speak with the power and the might of a first rate country instead of the wishy-washy language of diplomatic compromise." Daniel A. Darlington's Letter to the Editor, *Denver Post*

On February 1, 1979, amid great fanfare, exiled cleric Ayatollah Ruhollah Khomeini landed in Tehran. The return of the leader of the revolution to his home country was one of the final markers of the Iranian Revolution, a national phenomenon that had global implications. The Iranian Revolution of 1979 has been described as an epochal event, called the peak of 20th century Islamic revivalism and revitalization, and analyzed as the one key incident that continues to impact politics across Iran, the Middle East, and the even the world as a whole. As a phenomenon that led to the creation of the first modern Islamic Republic in the world, the revolution marked the victory of Islam over secular politics, and Iran quickly became the aspiring model for Islamic fundamentalists and revivalists across the globe, regardless of nationality, culture, or religious sect. When Ayatollah Khomeini was declared ruler in December 1979 and the judicial system originally modeled on that of the West was swiftly replaced by one purely based on Islamic law, much of the world was in shock that such a religiously driven revolution could succeed so quickly, especially when it had such sweeping consequences beyond the realm of religion.

Furthermore, while the focus of the revolution was primarily about Islam, the revolution was also colored by disdain for the West, distaste for autocracy, and a yearning for religious and cultural identity. This point was driven home on November 4, 1979 when Iranians stormed the U.S. embassy and took dozens of Americans hostage, sparking a crisis that would last for the rest of President Jimmy Carter's term. A few Americans escaped the embassy and hid in Tehran before being extracted (a mission that was recently adapted into the movie *Argo*), but for nearly 450 days, the crisis remained at the forefront of America's daily life, and aside from an embarrassing failed rescue mission, the administration seemed uncertain over how to approach the crisis and protect the American hostages. Eventually, all of the hostages were freed on the day Ronald Reagan was inaugurated as president in 1981, but the Iran hostage crisis had far reaching ramifications that have lasted to this day. Most notably, formal diplomatic contact between the United States and Iran ended, and no American embassy is open in that country nearly 35 years later.

For anyone born during the 1960s, the Iran Hostage Crisis marked a change in American identity both as people and a nation. Those born in earlier decades had little to no understanding of radical Islam, and those born later could not conceive of a world without it. Some would say that the crisis was ultimately a good thing, in that it ushered Ronald Reagan into the White House and thus led to the fall of Communism, while others would say that it was a harbinger of doom, a demonstration that even as one geopolitical foe declined, another was on the rise. Some say America was singled out because it was seen as too strong, others because it was seen as too weak. The bottom line is that, while no one knows what might have been done to prevent it, everyone has an idea about how it might have been ended sooner.

The Iran Hostage Crisis: The History of the Standoff that Ended Diplomatic Contacts Between the United States and Iran chronicles the tense chain of events that helped end Jimmy Carter's presidency and produced a diplomatic freeze between the U.S. and Iran. Along with pictures and a bibliography, you'll learn about the hostage crisis like never before.

The Iran Hostage Crisis: The History of the Standoff that Ended Diplomatic Contacts Between the United States and Iran

About Charles River Editors

Introduction

Chapter 1: The Road to Revolution

After the Islamic invasion of the 7th century and Iran's conquer by Muslim Arabs, Islam became the dominant religion of the nation. Though Sunni Islam was initially more dominant, the establishment of the Safavid Dynasty by Shah Ismail I in 1501 subsequently led to the forced conversion of Iran from Sunni to Shi'a Islam, and all other religious and forms of Islam were effectively suppressed and banned.[1] The declaration of Shi'ism as the state religion led to the vicious and often violent state-sponsored campaign to persuade the predominantly Sunni population to convert, by force if necessary. Prominent Sunni clerics were persecuted or killed, and hundreds of Shi'ite scholars were brought in from neighboring countries to form a new religious elite.

A portrait of Shah Ismail I

---

[1] "Safavid Empire (1501-1722)," *BBC Religions*, last modified September 7, 2009, http://www.bbc.co.uk/religion/religions/islam/history/safavidempire_1.shtml.

For centuries, the Shi'ite *ulama*, or clerics, enjoyed a prominent role in Iranian society. It was they who ran religious schools, arbitrated disputes, acted as mediators and judges, managed the charity of endowments, and oversaw the well-being of the community. In this way, clerics in Iran historically enjoyed a role beyond their religious obligations, and they were traditionally viewed not only as religious advisors and intermediaries to God but also as political, economic, and social figures who were essential to the overall welfare of society.

The Qajar dynasty was Iran's ruling dynasty from 1794-1925, and it was during this period that the *ulama* developed and strengthened their authority, status, and power, both in the religious and political realms. The rise of these Shi'ite clerics came at the expense of the isolation of other Islamic sects, such as the Sunnis and Sufi orders, and Iran increasingly became closely tied to the Shi'ite branch of Islam.

In essence, while *ulama* were historically religious and legal scholars engaged in the study of Islamic jurisprudence and *sharia* law, it was in Iran that these *ulama* expanded beyond the judicial and religious spheres they had historically occupied, and they ventured into the political arena to wield significant power and authority over state governance – much more so than the *ulama* of other Middle Eastern countries. Much of this was due to the Qajar rulers, who relied on the *ulama* as providers of religious legitimacy to secure the power of the dynasty. The founder of the Qajar dynasty, Aqa Muhammad Khan, and his successor, Fath Ali Shah, both actively engaged the *ulama* and allowed them great freedoms in return for a seal of legitimacy for their rule. Thus, by the end of the Qajar dynasty in 1925, these clerics had gained significant political powers, cementing their position as key components of rulership in Iran.[2]

The *ulama* as a political force only continued to grow, so much so that they became "Iran's first line of defense against colonialism."[3] It was the *ulama* who led the resistance against foreign influence in Iran, and it was the *ulama* who fought for the preservation of Iranian culture, religion, and self-rule in the face of foreign insurgency into the country during the 1800s. In 1890, when a tobacco concession was granted by the Shah of Iran to Great Britain, it was not the merchants or community leaders but the *ulama* who led the mass protests against the concession, as many of them had economic interests in tobacco that was growing on land funded by endowments.[4] Bazaars closed down following the *ulama's* calls for a strike, and many clerics stopped teaching and shut down schools. The protests culminated in a widely-obeyed December 1891 decree issued by Grand Ayatollah Mirza Hassan Shirazi, the highest religious authority in Iran, prohibiting the use of tobacco. By January 1892, the Shah had no choice but to cancel the concession.[5]

[2] Ahmad Kazemi Moussavi, "The Basis and Nature of Ulama's Authority in Qajar Iran," *Foundation For Iranian Studies*, http://fis-iran.org/en/irannameh/volxv/ulama-authority.

[3] Vali Nasr, *The Shia Revival: How Conflicts within Islam Will Shape the Future* (New York: W. W. Norton & Company, Inc., 2007), 117.

[4] Nikki R. Keddie, *Religion and Rebellion in Iran: The Tobacco Protest of 1891-92* (London: Frank Cass & Co. Ltd, 1966), 65.

The *ulama's* key role during the Tobacco Movement (1891-1892) was only one instance of their influence. Subsequent examples include their role in the Constitutional Revolution of 1905-1911, which has been investigated at length by many scholars and researchers,[6] and naturally, the political strength and influence the *ulama* possessed played a major role in the Iranian Revolution. To a degree that was unseen in any other Muslim country in the world, these clerics held sway over millions of people, who considered the clerics to be the ultimate source of morality, political legitimacy, and religious authority.

In 1921, a military commander named Reza Khan organized a coup against the ruling regime and ousted the last Qajar Shah. Reza Khan subsequently changed the country's name from Persia to Iran, and in 1925, he adopted the Pahlavi surname and established the Pahlavi dynasty.[7] Mohammad Reza Shah Pahlavi, son of Reza Shah and future ruler of Iran, wistfully wrote in his autobiography that his father's "coup was carried out with such dispatch and so few casualties that the commander of British forces in Persia, General Ironside, is said to have told friends that 'Reza Khan is the only man capable of saving Iran.'"[8]

[5] Roy Mottahedeh, *The Mantle of the Prophet: Religion and Politics in Iran* (Oxford: Oneworld Publications, 2000), 218.

[6] For example, see: Mohammad H. Faghfoory, "The Ulama-State Relations in Iran: 1921-1941," *International Journal of Middle East Studies* 19, no. 4 (Nov 1987): 413-432.

[7] Marvin E. Gettleman and Stuart Schaar, ed. *The Middle East and Islamic World Reader* (New York: Grove Press, 2003), 107.

[8] Mohammad Reza Pahlavi, *Answer to History* (New York: Stein & Day, 1980), 50-51.

Reza Shah Pahlavi

Reza Shah, whom the people initially had high hopes for, eventually disappointed many. Reform-minded liberals who had hoped for the establishment of an effective and modern parliamentary regime, and the *ulama,* who were expecting the continuation of the powers and high status they enjoyed during the Qajar dynasty, soon found that Reza Shah had no interest in actualizing anyone's visions but his own. He had no intention of upholding the status of the clerics; in fact, Reza Shah undermined the *ulama's* legitimacy by appointing secularists to key government positions and establishing ties with the West, which was considered anathema to both the reformists and the religious clerics.

Moreover, Reza Shah was an ambitious optimist who had great plans for the economic revitalization and modernization of his country, but for his plans to come into fruition, he believed that he needed a strong and centralized government composed of educated and intelligent advisors instead of clerics, who were knowledgeable in religion but not so much in state governance. As a great admirer of Kemal Ataturk, who in 1923 had established a secular modern republic in neighboring Turkey, Reza Shah dreamed of Iran as its own modern republic, free from religious and ethnic divides and united by common patriotism for a secular regime. Reza Shah consequently sent hundreds of Iranians, including his son, to Europe for education and training, and he led the establishment of a modernized national public education system. A new judiciary system modeled on that of France was introduced, and compulsory primary education was mandated across the country.[9] Thus, from the establishment of the new Iran to the 1940s, Reza Shah's development projects led to the urbanization and industrialization of Iran.

Naturally, Reza Shah's efforts to reform Iran into a modern republic were met with great opposition from various interest groups in the country. Reza found difficulties maneuvering between the various powerful political and economic players in his country, including politicians concerned about their future place in a changing government, merchants with various economic interests, and other ethnic groups like the Kurds, Azerbaijanis, and Baluchistanis. However, it was with the *ulama* that he clashed most significantly once the religious clerics were suddenly deprived of their long-held privileges, status, and power. Mohammad Shah wrote that "had my father not curtailed political efforts of certain clerics, the tasks which he had undertaken would have been far more difficult." It was not that Reza Shah was irreligious, or lacked spiritual faith; he quite simply believed that "in the twentieth century, it was impossible for a nation to survive in obscurantism. True spirituality should exist over and above politics and economics."[10] Reza Shah's efforts thus significantly, if not completely, reduced the *ulama's* authority in secular matters of state governance. Gaining strength in the clerics' stead were the newly formed middle and industrial working classes.

Despite the unrest at home, Reza Shah's aspirations ultimately crumbled when World War II swept across the globe. Reza Shah, who had been sympathetic to Nazi Germany[11], was consequently deposed by invading British forces for his pro-Axis sympathies and exiled to South Africa. Upon his abdication, he gave his seat of power to his son, Mohammad Reza Shah Pahlavi. Reza Shah died soon after, on July 26, 1944, in South Africa.

---

[9] Ibid., 51-55.

[10] Ibid., 55.

[11] Mohammad Reza Shah has consistently denied his father's alleged pro-Nazi sympathies. See the Shah's autobiography, *Answer to History,* p. 66 onwards for more details.

Mohammad Reza Shah Pahlav

On September 16, 1941, at the young age of 21, Mohammad Reza Shah ascended to the throne.[12] Unlike his father, or perhaps in fear of being accused of pro-Axis sympathies as his father was, Mohammad Reza Shah was more willing to aid in the Allied war effort. With the Shah's blessing, Iran was used by American and British forces as a shipping conduit for supplies being sent to the Soviet Union during the war.[13] Though the Shah was able to boost his ties with Western powers because of this, in the eyes of much of the Iranian population, Mohammad Reza Shah was largely viewed as a puppet of Western powers, and his legitimacy and ability to rule

---

[12] Spencer C. Tucker, ed. *The Encyclopedia of Middle East Wars: The United States in the Persian Gulf, Afghanistan, and Iraq Conflicts* (Santa Barbara: ABC-CLIO, 2010), 1033.

[13] Tucker, *Encyclopedia of Middle East Wars*, 1033.

increasingly came into question.

The foreign-educated, pampered, yet idealistic young man – passionate about his country but with a mind for the outside world – inherited the governance of a country that was increasingly growing restless with the unprecedented reforms placed upon it. In the post-war liberal climate, a democratically elected Majlis (parliament) appointed an ambitious and aggressive nationalist, Mohammed Mossadegh, as prime minister in 1950. The Mossadegh government was committed to the economic revitalization of Iran and quickly sought to nationalize the Iranian oil industry, which had been controlled by the British company Anglo-Persian Oil Company (AIOC) since a 1933 concession agreement with Reza Shah, a bitter memory for many Iranians. In March 1951, the Majlis unanimously voted to nationalize AIOC and its holdings, which led to a global boycott of Iranian crude, the country's primary export and the main source of state wealth. As the Iranian economy plummeted and national unrest grew, a power struggle between Mossadegh and the Shah led to Mohammad Reza Shah fleeing the country into exile in 1953.

Mossadegh

It was only after a CIA-orchestrated coup effectively ousted Mossadegh and toppled his government that Mohammad Reza Shah was able to return to Tehran and resume his role as absolute monarch, with the blessings of the U.S. and Great Britain. The Majlis was stripped of its powers, and foreign oil companies resumed their work in Iran. That Mohammad Reza so quickly lost his seat of power was an embarrassment for the Shah, and the fact that it required the help of the CIA and Western powers to regain his position would remain as a lasting memory in the minds of his people. It would also come back to haunt him.

Mohammad Reza Shah was highly in favor of the U.S., establishing close political ties with the Western country, but he was also restrictive and oppressive in his ways, favoring landowners and the military at the expense of the rest of the population and repressing any opposition to his rule.[14] Through mass arms transfers from his new ally, the U.S., and with the help of American military trainers and advisors, the Shah built one of the most well-equipped, highly trained, and powerful armed forces in the region.

Meanwhile, the secret police that he formed, SAVAK, was given great authority to hunt down dissidents and forcibly prevent the population from voicing opposition. Thus, by the mid-1970s, most of the opposition, including leftist reformists, religious leaders, liberal critics, and nationalists, had been silenced through assassinations, unlawful indefinite detentions, and exile.[15] It was this repression that led to the formation of a more furtive kind of opposition that took root in mosques across the country, and eventually, the Shah's most vociferous critic, Ruhollah Khomeini, was exiled from the country in the mid-1960s.

[14] Gettleman and Schaar, *The Middle East and Islamic World Reader*, 108.
[15] Stephen Zunes, "The Iranian Revolution (1977-1979)," *Nonviolent Conflict*, April 2009, http://www.nonviolent-conflict.org/index.php/movements-and-campaigns/movements-and-campaigns-summaries?sobi2Task=sobi2Details&catid=315&sobi2Id=23.

Khomeini

In 1963, Mohammad Reza Shah launched a national program he called the White Revolution, which had been approved for implementation by a national referendum in January of that year. The five-point program was built upon the purported overarching goal that the five minimum human needs would be met for all citizens of Iran: health, food, clothing, housing, and education.[16] As Mohammad Reza Shah wrote in his autobiography, "If our nation wished to remain in the circle of dynamic, progressive and free nations of the world, it had no alternative but to completely alter the archaic order of society, and to structure its future on a new order compatible with the vision and needs of the day. This required a deep and fundamental revolution which would put an end to injustice, tyranny, exploitation, and reactionary forces which impeded progress. This revolution had to be based on spiritual principles and religious

---

[16] Pahlavi, *Answer to History*, 101.

beliefs, and the preservation of individual and social freedoms."[17]

Western nations, unsurprisingly, applauded the Shah's new program and lauded his efforts. The Shah received a personal note of congratulations from President John F. Kennedy, and in August 1967, U.S. President Lyndon B. Johnson declared that "the changes in Iran represent very genuine progress. Through your White Revolution…Iran has risen to the challenge of new times and new generations…without violence, and without any bloodshed."[18]

Though some significant progress came out of the White Revolution, such as women's suffrage, increased literacy, and improved infrastructure and technology, this supposed cultural revolution ultimately proved to be more of an attempt by the power-holding political elite to preempt an actual revolution than anything else. They were wary of an increasingly politically conscious population and hoped to merely maintain the political status quo.

It is difficult to pinpoint a single and direct cause of the Iranian Revolution, as it is with most other revolutions and similar world events. The revolution was highly controversial in both its causes and its consequences, not to mention the surprise it created across the world since it was so unexpected, quick, and impactful.

Few expected the Shah's regime, which had broad international support, a powerful and disciplined military, and state wealth, to struggle so much with popular protests, and even fewer could have even guessed that such a regime would crumble in mere months. As one historian noted, "[The Iranian Revolution was] unique in the annals of modern world history in that it brought to power not a new social group equipped with political parties and secular ideologies, but a traditional clergy armed with mosque pulpits and claiming the divine right to supervise all temporal authorities, even the country's highest elected representatives."[19]

The Iranian Revolution transpired relatively quickly for one that led to such significant changes, and the protest movements that had begun to organize in the mid- to late 1970s flowered into full-fledged demonstrations and riots in a matter of mere months.

The events and causes of the revolution discussed before were building to a crescendo during the later years of the decade. The Shah's White Revolution and policies of modernization, Westernization, and industrialization were underway, but this was also the era of significant steps for democratization and human and civil rights across the world, led by President Jimmy Carter. It was during this decade of global political liberalization that the Shah gradually began to loosen his grip, and even the much-feared SAVAK lessened its degree of surveillance and oppression. In the 1970s, Mohammad Reza Shah invited international human rights organizations to Iran to inspect prisons and observe the trials of his political opponents, and he

[17] Ibid.
[18] Ibid., 102.
[19] Ervand Abrahamian, *Iran Between Two Revolutions* (Princeton: Princeton University Press, 1982), 430-435.

also announced that parliamentary elections "that would grant the electorate a free choice" would be held in 1978.[20]

The opposition quickly took advantage of the political liberalization by seizing on its chance to organize, and by 1977, the beginnings of protest were already simmering. Over the course of several months, intellectuals and scholars began testing the waters of the Shah's ostensible liberalization process by tentatively beginning to publish their grievances and criticisms in the form of essays, letters, and pamphlets. Organizations and political parties that had long operated underground began to emerge above ground, further testing the limits of liberalization. New student groups and human rights organizations were founded, advocating for President Carter's principles of universal human rights to be implemented in Iran. These groups' "very existence implied an enormous change in the political environment, and they provided important foci for the articulation of grievances and the beginnings of expression of public opinion."[21]

Ironically, it was not religious Islamic groups that first initiated these protests, meaning the prelude to the revolution was largely secular. Leftist groups such as the Iranian Writers Association began demonstrating, denouncing the Shah's rule, and calling for full liberalization, and in the fall of 1977, thousands gathered at the Goethe Institute in Tehran, led by the leftist intellectual Saeed Soltanpour.[22] A sit-in ensued, and the protest eventually turned violent as demonstrators clashed with security forces, leading to several deaths and dozens injured. Though the Iranian Writers Association's contribution to the revolution ended here, it was decisive in that it was the first spark and the biggest sign of things to come; the association "played a crucial role by attacking the government in the initial stage of the conflict when it appeared unassailable."[23]

In October 1977, Mostafa Khomeini, the son of Ayatollah Khomeini, died of a heart attack in Najaf, Iraq. Like his father, Mostafa was a respected cleric in Iraq, and his sudden death and the suspicious circumstances surrounding it brought rise to whispers of foul play and a Shah-sanctioned assassination, which eventually transformed into outright accusations that SAVAK had murdered Mostafa. Khomeini himself, who had initially responded to Mostafa's death calmly and quietly, began shouting anti-Shah slogans at Mostafa's memorial and declaring his son a martyr. In Qom and in Tehran, clerics and Khomeini's supporters gathered to deliver speeches and demonstrations. The police eventually intervened and dispersed the crowd as the protests turned more radical,[24] but demonstrations continued throughout the year, and the number of those arrested continued to grow. Mostafa's death spawned mass political rallies and

[20] Daniel Philip Ritter, "Why the Iranian Revolution Was Nonviolent: Internationalized Social Change and the Iron Cage of Liberalism" (PhD diss., University of Texas at Austin, 2010), 201-202.
[21] Ritter, "Why the Iranian Revolution Was Nonviolent," 203.
[22] Ibid., 206-207.
[23] Misagh Parsa, *Social Origins of the Iranian Revolution* (New Brunswick, NJ: Rutgers University Press, 1989), 179.
[24] Michael Axworthy, *Revolutionary Iran: A History of the Islamic Republic* (London: Penguin Group, 2013), 101-102.

vociferous demonstrations, and for many Iranians, this was their first exposure to Ayatollah Khomeini and his views. Khomeini would later attribute his son's death to God due to the way it helped forward the cause of revolution.

Mostafa Khomeini

By January 1978, protests were intensifying, with hard-line students, Khomeini supporters, and clerics marching through the streets of Qom. In response, the Shah once again reverted back to repressive measures by shrinking the political space available to the opposition. On January 7, 1978, an article that slandered Khomeini as a British agent and a homosexual of Indian origins was published in the national newspaper *Ittila'at*. Though no author was attributed to the article, the people quickly concluded that the government was undoubtedly involved. Khomeini's supporters reacted vehemently, and the following day, thousands of Islamic teachers, students, clerics, and Khomeini supporters marched the streets of Qom. In conjunction with that, the Bazaari merchants shut down their shops. Security forces clashed with the protestors, and approximately 70 protestors lost their lives, while over 400 were injured. [25]

The Shah's regime continued to disadvantage itself by making irreversible blunders that contributed to the revolution instead of preventing it. On August 19, 1978, the Cinema Rex in the oil city of Abadan, in southwestern Iran, was set ablaze. At least 377 people, and possibly more, lost their lives that day, and the government swiftly blamed the opposition without providing justifications. The details surrounding the blaze were suspicious, and the presence of SAVAK agents at the cinema did nothing to stop the rumors that the intelligence agency had orchestrated the fire as a false flag operation.[26] The doors of the cinema had been barred, and remnants of

[25] Ritter, "Why the Iranian Revolution Was Nonviolent," 207-208.
[26] Daniel L. Byman, "The Rise of Low-Tech Terrorism," *Brookings,* May 6, 2007,

chemical agents were found, indicating that this was an intentional crime. Though later findings concluded that revolutionary students had started the fire, since the circumstances of the tragedy were so murky, the opposition took advantage by carefully crafting the belief that SAVAK was behind the fire.[27] This was a major blow to the regime, which had failed to come up with an organized and convincing response to the accusations, and the incident sparked protests across the country.

Picture of a protest held in Tehran

The sheer number of protestors and the non-violent, dignified, yet starkly adamant nature of the protests served as the final wake-up call for the Shah. This was no longer a crazed uprising or a chaotic opposition movement that could be wrestled under control and subdued. The crowds were peaceful, restrained, and determined, and Khomeini's portraits filled the streets. Many Iranians had already taken down their pictures of Mohammad Reza Shah, and foreign advisors and workers were leaving the country, to the extent that by early January 1979, the number of Americans in Iran dropped from 58,000 to just 12,000.[28] Desertions were now rampant in the Iranian army, and soldiers joined the opposition.[29] The message was clear: the Shah must go.

---

http://www.brookings.edu/research/articles/2007/05/06terrorism-byman.

[27] Glenn Eldon Curtis and Eric Hooglund, ed. *Iran: A Country Study* (Washington, DC: Government Printing Office, 2008), 48.

[28] Axworthy, *Revolutionary Iran*, 123-124.

[29] Ritter, "Why the Iranian Revolution Was Nonviolent," 234.

Pictures of the protests

In mid-December, the Shah began talks with the moderate opposition and reached out to several of its leaders, including Shapour Bakhtiar. The Shah offered Bakhtiar an opportunity to form a government, and Bakhtiar agreed, provided that the Shah leave the country. On January 3, 1979, Bakhtiar secured a vote of confidence from the Majlis and formed a cabinet. The Shah left

Iran on January 16, and the streets of Iran were filled with celebration. Statues of the Shah were pulled down, and processions carrying Khomeini banners and waving Khomeini's pictures filled Tehran.

Bakhtiar

A picture of revolutionaries pulling down a statue of Reza Shah

A picture of protesters pulling down a statue of the Shah

On January 17, 1979, President Jimmy Carter said in a press conference, "As you know, the Shah has left Iran; he says for a vacation. How long he will be out of Iran, we have no way to determine. Future events and his own desires will determine that. He's now in Egypt, and he will later come to our own country. But we would anticipate and would certainly hope that our good relationships with Iran will continue in the future. ... I have confidence in the Iranian people to restore a stable government and to restore their economic circumstances for the future." The president was then asked about how the United States would work with Khomeini, who seemed to be behind the unrest that led to the Shah's overthrow. While at that time the Ayatollah was still out of the country, it seemed likely that he would soon step into the power vacuum created when the Shah left. Carter explained, "We have not communicated directly with Mr. Khomeini.

Our views have been expressed publicly that he support stability and an end to bloodshed in Iran and, no matter what his deep religious convictions might be—and I don't doubt their sincerity—that he permit the government that has now been established by the legal authorities in Iran, and under the Constitution, to have a chance to succeed. We do know that the Iranian military and many of the religious and political opponents to the Shah have given their pledge of support to the Bahktiar government. And that's our hope. ... We have no intention, neither ability nor desire, to interfere in the internal affairs of Iran, and we certainly have no intention of permitting other nations to interfere in the internal affairs of Iran. ... We have some existing contracts for delivery of weapons to Iran, since sometimes the deliveries take as long as 5 years after the orders are placed. ... After the Iranian Government is stable, after it assuages the present disturbances in Iran, then I'm sure they'll let us know how they want to carry out future military needs of their own country. It is important to Iran, for their own security and for the independence of the people of Iran, that a strong and stable military be maintained. And I believe that all the leaders of Iran whom I have heard discuss this matter agree with the statement that I've just made."

Carter

Just days later, on January 20, 1979, Khomeini announced that he was returning to Tehran. As part of his liberalization efforts, Bakhtiar had initially stated that Khomeini was welcome to return, but he chose to close down Mehrabad airport to prevent Khomeini's homecoming, fearing that the Ayatollah's presence would only further destabilize the country. This proved to be a dire mistake, because between January 26 and 28, as troops worked to shut down the airport, several protestors were killed as they tried to prevent the closure. The deaths were condemned, and Bakhtiar was declared to be just another corrupt leader willing to kill demonstrators at the behest of the Shah. The airport reopened on January 31,[30] and the gates were open for Khomeini's

[30] Axworthy, *Revolutionary Iran,* 130.

return.

On February 1, 1979, Ayatollah Khomeini landed in Tehran on a chartered Air France plane. Amid a rapturous welcome from millions of Iranians, Khomeini announced that he was appointing Mehdi Bazargan as prime minister of a provisional government – one that competed with that of Shapour Bakhtiar. The army, Western powers, and the people began abandoning Bakhtiar's government en masse.[31]

A picture of Khomeini's return

With the fall of Shapour Bakhtiar and his government, Ayatollah Khomeini was free to consolidate his power and build his envisioned state. Within days of the success of the revolution, a flurry of political and journalistic activities arose; political parties were formed, new newspapers and media outlets emerged, and social groups were established. Khomeini recognized the outpouring of activity in this environment of victory and newfound freedom, and he quickly understood that it must be controlled. Nonetheless, he also understood that sudden oppression would be detrimental in such a highly charged environment.

Khomeini's initial caution led to conflicts and power struggles both within the ruling

---

[31] Ibid., 130.

government and between the government and other organizations. Khomeini's subsequent consolidation of power was an arduous process, but one that significantly strengthened his position to an irreversible degree.

Two weeks after Khomeini returned to Tehran and seized power, Carter addressed the development by saying, "Over the past several months, we have observed closely the events unfolding there. Our objective has been and is a stable and independent Iran which maintains good relations with the United States of America. ... We hope that the differences that have divided the people of Iran for so many months can now be ended. As has been the case throughout this period, we have been in touch with those in control of the Government of Iran, and we stand ready to work with them. Our goals are now, as they have been for the past few months, to ensure the safety of Americans in Iran, to minimize bloodshed and violence, to ensure that Iran is militarily capable of protecting her independence and her territorial integrity, to prevent interference or intervention in the internal affairs of Iran by any outside power, and to honor the will of the Iranian people."

At first, Carter refused to allow the exiled Shah to come to the United States. However, no matter what his political views of the Iranian situation, Carter found it impossible to refuse the Shah's plea to come to America for medical treatment for his advanced cancer. The Shah arrived on October 22, and on October 24, a *United Press International* article reported, "The exiled shah of Iran was hospitalized in serious condition in New York Tuesday for treatment of what U.S. State Department officials described as cancer. State Department officials in Washington said European and American doctors examined Shah Mohammed Reza Pahlavi and discovered he was suffering from a "malignant tumor" — a form of cancer — and a blocked bile duct. ... The 59-year-old Shah, who has lived under constant threat of assassination since he left Iran in January, thanked President Carter and the government for letting him enter the country. The Shah was admitted to New York Hospital-Cornell Medical Center. In Washington, State Department officials said the Shah was admitted to the United States strictly for medical reasons and would return to Mexico after American doctors had finished treating him. Department spokesman Hodding Carter said the United States had informed Iran that the Shah would enter the country, but Carter declined to reveal Tehran's response."

This humanitarian decision would prove to have tragic consequences just two weeks later.

Chapter 2: A Symbolic Stand

"Everybody, including the Students Following the Line of the Imam, expected the U.S. embassy takeover to be a short-lived affair. The students had only brought enough food for themselves to last three days. They wanted to make a symbolic stand. ... Self-consciously, the students perceived the embassy takeover as 'propaganda of the deed.' They had no clear demands. They really were just students and they did not expect to find themselves in the middle of an immensely complicated, chaotic, and seemingly endless factional power struggle within

Iran in which their little escapade would take on immense weight. In Iran, the hostage-taking became a singularly vital episode in a tale of national self-determination and revolutionary grit. President Carter, who was at Camp David when he received word of the embassy takeover from Secretary Vance, assumed that the proper Iranian authorities would exert control as they had in February and put a stop to the student militants' actions. Carter's chief of staff, Hamilton Jordan, apprised of the situation at 4:30 a.m., groggily told the president's secretary, over the phone, to make sure that Carter paid attention to the incident. ... Jordan believed that the White House had a simple political story to tell: Carter stands tall during the crisis and shows voters he can lead the nation." – David Farber, *Taken Hostage: The Iran Hostage Crisis and America's First Encounter with Radical Islam* (2005)

Back in Iran, students who had been following the Ayatollah were furious that the Americans had offered sanctuary to their hated former leader, and large crowds of them gathered outside the U.S. embassy in Teheran to protest the decision. Ebrahim Asgharzadeh, one of the students who participated in the protests, later explained, "We felt insulted -- our revolution, our people -- and so there was a rebellion. A measure was needed to be taken that was effective, that could impact the world public opinion. We were not radical students. We were revolutionary students, in the sense that we were defending our country, our people, our nation...What the students did for the first two or three days, it was a student activity. It was meant to protest, something that American students did many times on the streets to protest the Vietnam War."

For the students, the 1953 coup was only something they had heard about from their parents or learned about in school, but for others in Tehran, it was recent and well-remembered history. Ibrahim Yazdi, Khomeini's foreign minister, later said in an interview, "You must keep in your mind … What happened in August 1953 in Iran. That the Americans and the British … made a military coup against the national government of Dr. Mossadegh and the Shah … fled the country. They brought him back. The moment that they wanted to take the Shah to the United States, all these memories came to the mind of our people. They say 'oh no', that's again the same story."

Moreover, it seemed to some Iranians that the United States was indeed gearing up for another coup, likely to oust Khomeini and reinstate the Shah. William Daugherty, a CIA agent who found himself taken hostage, noted, "To the ever-suspicious Iranian radicals, the admission of the Shah for medical treatment was a sham designed to hide a conspiracy aimed at overthrowing their revolutionary government. To add more fuel to the fire, Prime Minister Mehdi Bazargan and Foreign Minister Ibrahim Yazdi (a graduate of a US medical school who had practiced his profession in the United States, and who held a Permanent Resident Alien green card) met briefly with National Security Adviser Brzezinski in Algiers on 1 November 1979, during the celebration of Algeria's independence day. In this meeting, which was not publicized in Algiers, the Shah and the future of US—Iranian relations were discussed."

Meanwhile, for those inside the embassy, things were tense but life went on as usual. A posting to anywhere as unsettled as Iran was always dangerous, but it was a situation they had come to accept. After all, there were American Marines stationed at the gates to keep out intruders and a network of spies always gathering information to warn them if anything was being planned. Charles Scott, who worked at the embassy, described what living in the bubble was like at the time: "We had no feeling for the view of the vast majority of the Iranian people at the time. Because they believed as an article of faith that if the Shah came to the United States, it would usher in a series of events similar to those that had happened in 1953, when the CIA …assisted the pro-Shah demonstrators in overthrowing Mohammed Mossadegh and putting the Shah back on the Peacock throne. They believed that as an article of faith. Whether it was true or not is irrelevant."

November 4, 1979 seemed to begin like any other day for those in the embassy, and they busied themselves conducting all the normal activities associated with operating a federal bureaucracy. Some people were on the phone, others behind their desks, and several men and women were standing in the hall getting caught up on news from the previous evening. Outside the walls, it initially appeared that a large number of students were headed to nearby Tehran University to hold one of their frequent anti-American rallies, but this time, some of the students began to move away from the main group and surround the embassy.

Even as this activity picked up, none of the Americans considered it unusual. Tom Schaefer recalled, "It looked like a bunch of students this time were coming by. I was not even concerned that students were going by, until someone said 'They're getting through the gate.' I honestly felt that's all it was, it was a bunch of students. They probably just want to talk to us. And eventually we found that there was more than this because they were taking other American workers out of the outbuildings, blindfolding them, with guns to their heads, and that was my first indication really that this is more than just a student visit to our embassy, that this is serious."

However, before anyone knew what had happened, a mob of students stormed the main gate and came over the walls into the embassy compound. This set off a frenzy of activity in the embassy, much of it focusing on destroying potentially confidential papers. When a malfunctioning furnace couldn't be used to burn them, American staffers began shredding everything they could.

A picture of the shredded documents

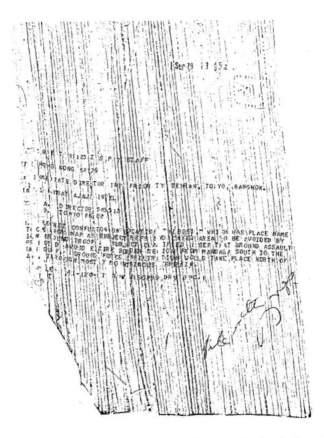

A picture of a shredded document woven back together by the Iranians

By early afternoon, they had complete control of the building and had blindfolded their hostages, parading them before reporters for all the world to see. The next day, a *United Press International* story reported, "Moslem students battled U.S. Marines for three hours and seized the U.S. embassy Sunday, taking 90 Americans hostage to press demands that the deposed shah be extradited to Iran to face Islamic justice. About 450 Moslem youths, who said they had tacit approval from Ayatollah Ruhollah Khomeini, stormed the embassy at 2 a.m. EST and "fought with embassy personnel" for three hours…The students seized some 90 American men, women and children and another 10 Iranians, the spokesman said. The protestors told reporters that Marines used teargas against them to try to prevent the takeover. 'But our people came equipped with wet handkerchiefs,' said a spokesman. He said the students faced the strongest opposition from Marines when they tried to take over what appeared to be a specially guarded room. 'Six men, guarding the room resisted our students until all documents inside the room were burned. The documents which were destroyed probably belonged to the CIA,' said the spokesman. The State Department in Washington said there was no indication the Americans were hurt. A special task force, headed by Assistant Secretary of State Harold Saunders, was established to handle the matter."

The article went on to quote the Iranian foreign minister, who insisted, "The action taken today by a group of our countrymen reflects the natural feelings of the Iranian nation towards the U.S. government's disregard on this issue. If the American authorities had respected the feeling of the Iranian people and realized the depth of the Iranian revolution, they would have at least refused to let the former Shah enter their country and would return his properties to Iran."

Although it would later come out that Khomeini did not know of the plan to take over the embassy, the students appeared to have the support of the current Iranian regime. The *UPI* report read, "The spokesman for the students said Khomeini's office in Qom had contacted the group and 'not opposed our action.' He said the Experts Assembly, currently processing Iran's new Islamic revolution, had passed a special motion approving the action." This assumption seemed to be confirmed the following morning when the Iranian government cancelled standing treaties with both the United States and the Soviet Union that would have allowed one or both of those governments to send troops into Iran to rescue the hostages.

A picture of students ripping up an American flag on November 5

A picture of the November 5 *Islamic Republican* **newspaper with the headline**
"Revolutionary occupation of U.S. embassy"

Chapter 3: The Months Went By

"At that point the American public believed fifty hostages were held by the Iranians—three other Americans were residing in a limbo state at the Iranian Foreign Ministry and six others were hiding in the Canadian embassy. The Carter administration kept the number of hostages unclear to protect the status of the Americans in Iran who were not held in the embassy. ... There had been some good news. Besides the thirteen hostages released in mid-November 1979, the six Americans who had made a successful run for it the day the hostages were taken and spent over two months hiding at the Canadian embassy had escaped in late January 1980 through the good offices of stalwart Canadian diplomats in Tehran." – David Farber, *Taken Hostage: The Iran Hostage Crisis and America's First Encounter with Radical Islam* (2005)

Seemingly overwhelmed by the turn of events, Carter remained publicly silent in the immediate wake of the embassy takeover, but on November 7 the president sent former Attorney General Ramsey Clark and Senate Intelligence Committee staff director William Miller to Iran to try to persuade Khomeini to order the hostages released. After the Ayatollah refused to meet with the Americans, Carter continued to work quietly behind the scenes until he finally made a public statement about the situation on November 12: "We continue to face a grave situation in Iran, where our Embassy has been seized and more than 60 American citizens continue to be held as hostages in an attempt to force unacceptable demands on our country. We're using every available channel to protect the safety of the hostages and to secure their release. Along with the families of the hostages, I have welcomed and I appreciate the restraint that has been shown by Americans during this crisis. We must continue to exhibit such constraint, despite the intensity of our emotions. The lives of our people in Iran are at stake. I must emphasize the gravity of the situation. It's vital to the United States and to every other nation that the lives of diplomatic personnel and other citizens abroad be protected and that we refuse to permit the use of terrorism and the seizure and the holding of hostages to impose political demands. No one should underestimate the resolve of the American Government and the American people in this matter."

Ramsey Clark

Carter then moved from the foreign policy matters to those that he was more comfortable with, namely domestic issues, including saving energy. He continued, "It is necessary to eliminate any suggestion that economic pressures can weaken our stand on basic issues of principle. Our position must be clear. I am ordering that we discontinue purchasing of any oil from Iran for delivery to this country. These events obviously demonstrate the extreme importance of reducing oil consumption here in the United States. I urge every American citizen and every American business to redouble efforts to curtail the use of petroleum products. This action will pose a real challenge to our country. It will be a test of our strength and of our determination. I directed Secretary Duncan to work with the Congress and with other Federal, State, and local officials, and with leaders of industry to develop additional measures to conserve oil and to cope with this new situation. We will strive to ensure equitable and fair distribution of petroleum products and to ensure a minimum of disruption of our Nation's economy. These American measures must be part of an effective international effort, and we will consult with our allies and with other oil-consuming nations about further actions to reduce oil consumption and oil imports."

When Carter was questioned about concerns that he had been wrong to let the Shah enter the United States, he replied, "The decision that I made, personally and without pressure from anyone, to carry out the principles of our country, to provide for the means of giving the Shah necessary medical assistance to save his life, was proper. At the same time, we notified the Government of Iran. We were assured by the Prime Minister and the Foreign Minister that our Embassy would be protected, and it was protected for several days, in spite of threats from outside. Then peremptorily, after Khomeini made an aggravating speech to the crowds in the street and withdrew protection from the Embassy, it was attacked successfully. The Embassy was protected by our people for the length of time possible without help from the host government. No embassy on Earth is a fortress that can withstand constant attacks by a mob, unless a host government comes to the rescue of the people within the embassy. But I took the right decision. I have no regrets about it nor apologies to make, because it did help to save a man's life, and it was compatible with the principles of our country."

On November 14, Carter took further action against Iran, telling Congress, "I have today exercised the authority granted [to the President] to block certain property or interests in property of the Government of Iran, its instrumentalities and controlled entities and the Central Bank of Iran. ...I have ordered blocked all property and interests in property of the Government of Iran, its instrumentalities and controlled entities and the Central Bank of Iran which are or become subject to the jurisdiction of the United States or which are or come within the possession of persons subject to the jurisdiction of the United States."

One of the biggest dilemmas the administration faced as a result of the crisis was that there was no comparable precedent in American history to which he could refer. Warren Christopher, then Deputy Secretary of State, explained, "While hostage situations are not unprecedented in the diplomatic community, in other cases host governments quite promptly have recognized their obligations under international law to protect foreign embassies against hostile elements in their populations. Here, however, the host government condoned and then embraced what the terrorists had done, and thus made the crime their own — an almost unprecedented act and one of extraordinary repugnance." Lloyd Cutler, who served President Carter as White House Counsel, pointed out, "In the beginning, of course, all our efforts were to ... assist the Iranian government in recapturing the embassy. We first thought of it very much like the Columbian situation that came along later or other terrorist seizures of embassies as happened in the Sudan, where the local government deplores what happened just as much as you do and does everything it can to bring it to an end."

Warren Christopher

Not surprisingly, many wanted Carter to take military action to rescue the hostages, but Carter was reluctant to take such a provocative action, at least at this early juncture. During one meeting in which the possibility was discussed, then CIA Director Stansfield Turner remembered, "The President reminded us of an incident in late 1978. When it had become clear that the Shah was in serious trouble, the President placed an aircraft carrier on alert to proceed into the Indian Ocean from the Pacific. The order immediately leaked, making it clear to the world we though the Shah was in so much trouble that the United States was bringing up force. That only exacerbated the Shah's problems. Now the President obviously did not want to risk a similar misfire."

Turner

That said, Carter did make some changes, including persuading the Shah to leave the United States and go to Panama. A few days later, the president noted, "We have emphasized over and over, not adequately yet, that there is no confrontation or schism between the world of Islam, the Moslem countries and our own country. This is not the point at all. And as far as the hostages are concerned, they are the only issue for us. It's not a proper time for us to discuss the wisdom or the role that the Shah played as a good or bad leader. It's not a proper time for us to get involved in a debate about whether he is or has been sick, or how sick, or where he goes, or to discuss the history of Iran. It's important, and we have recognized the importance of maintaining one issue foremost in our mind and in our national consciousness in our dealing with other countries, in our dealing with Iran, in our dealing with the United Nations, and that is the early and the safe release of the American hostages."

Fortunately, the end of January 1980 brought good news, as the *Associated Press* could report on the 28th, "Six American diplomats who had been hiding in friendly embassies in Tehran since Nov. 4 have escaped with the help of the Canadian embassy there…The diplomats were outside the embassy when it was seized and were able to hide until this past weekend, when Canada issued them false passports and got them out of Iran…They refused to say where all of the diplomats had hidden during their 12-week ordeal for fear that Iran would take reprisals against the embassies involved. Canada closed its embassy in Tehran and evacuated its small staff Monday, citing security concerns for the decision."

What the article did not say was that the CIA had been instrumental in planning and executing their escape. In fact, nearly two decades would pass before the information about the agency's involvement was made public. Known as the "Canadian Caper," the CIA plot successfully passed the stranded Americans off as part of a film crew making a movie called *Argo* to help get them extracted.

Pictures of promotional materials for the fake movie *Argo* used to bolster the cover

A picture of people on hand to welcome back the escapees

Following the Canadian Caper, the situation in Iran looked like it had reached a stalemate, and based on outward appearances, it seemed little was being done on either side to settle the fate of the hostages. The Shah left Panama in March and returned to Egypt, while the hostages remained imprisoned. One of them, Robert Ode, wrote in his journal on March 8, 1980, "Received a visit from an Iranian doctor who described himself as being with the Iranian "Red Lion Society" (similar to our Red Cross). ... I related to him in detail my heart condition, how it had caused partial loss of vision in my left eye; treatment I underwent...He listened to my heart and made some comments to the group of students which I couldn't understand after he had taken my name and age. He also took my blood pressure which was 150 over 100 - higher than its usual 120/80. I told him about my letter to Dr. Dustin and asked about the possibility of being released because of my age and physical condition. His only comment was 'If God wills!' The doctor was accompanied by still [cameramen] and TV cameramen and several of the students. The cameramen took pictures over my objections."

Ode and the others were frequently interviewed or treated in front of cameras, used again and again for propaganda purposes to show the good treatment they were providing to the Americans. A few days later, Ode noted, "Our room was visited by an English-speaking Iranian girl…together with a TV camera crew. She said they wanted pictures of all the hostages as a 'souvenir' for the students' files. I doubted this and objected to having the photos taken. … I let them proceed with me. I was required to state my name, position at the Embassy and when I had arrived in Iran. This was spoken into a microphone for sound on tape. … About this time, demonstrators were in the street in front of the Embassy (opposite our room) with amplifiers at full volume with one man shouting at the top of his voice leading a crowd in organized chants such as something like 'Allah-ho' to which the crowd would reply 'Ak-bar' (Is Greater) and 'Khomeini' with the crowd replying 'Rak-bar' (Is Great). These and other chants had been continuing around the clock for about four days, only quieting down a bit between perhaps 3:00 and 5:00 a.m.! The leader had become so hoarse from his constant yelling that his voice was breaking!"

A picture of blindfolded hostages during the crisis

The hostages continued to be used for propaganda purposes in March, and on March 13 and 14, Ode recorded in his journal, "Just at lunch time on March 13 we were told we were to be taken out of doors in the sunshine which was beautiful for a walk and could eat our lunch outdoors. However, this was not convenient so we didn't go that day. Then about 11:00 a.m. on March 14, I was blindfolded (as usual), taken outdoors and placed in a car and driven to the enclosure of the Embassy residence where we sometimes were taken for exercise. There was an 'exercise bike' in the yard. I was the only hostage there. I sat on the bike for about 10 minutes and a photographer took some color and black and white photos…. Sunshine was warm and lovely but I was there only about 10 minutes, obviously this was only for photographic (propaganda) purposes and not for my benefit!"

In April, President Carter decided to try to increase the financial pressure on Iran to prompt a release. In explaining his decision, he said, "Ever since Iranian terrorists imprisoned American Embassy personnel in Tehran early in November, these 50 men and women—their safety, their health, and their future—have been our central concern. We've made every effort to obtain their release on honorable, peaceful, and humanitarian terms, but the Iranians have refused to release them or even to improve the inhumane conditions under which these Americans are being held captive. The events of the last few days have revealed a new and significant dimension in this matter. The militants controlling the Embassy have stated they are willing to turn the hostages over to the Government of Iran, but the Government has refused to take custody of the American hostages. This lays bare the full responsibility of the Ayatollah Khomeini and the Revolutionary Council for the continued illegal and outrageous holding of the innocent hostages. The Iranian Government can no longer escape full responsibility by hiding behind the militants at the Embassy."

Carter then went on to outline a series of decisions designed to turn up the heat on Iran in hopes of facilitating the hostages' return. The first move, he said, was that "the United States of America is breaking diplomatic relations with the Government of Iran. The Secretary of State has informed the Government of Iran that its Embassy and consulates in the United States are to be closed immediately. All Iranian diplomatic and consular officials have been declared persona non grata and must leave this country by midnight tomorrow." Next, he said his administration would "put into effect official sanctions prohibiting exports from the United States to Iran…. Although shipment of food and medicine were not included in the U.N. Security Council vote, it is expected that exports even of these items to Iran will be minimal or nonexistent."

Carter also slapped financial sanctions against Iran: "[T]he Secretary of Treasury will make a formal inventory of the assets of the Iranian Government, which were frozen by my previous order, and also will make a census or an inventory of the outstanding claims of American citizens and corporations against the Government of Iran. This accounting of claims will aid in designing a program against Iran for the hostages, for the hostage families, and other U.S. claimants."

Finally, he made it clear that those visiting the United States from Iran were no longer welcome: "[T]he Secretary of Treasury [State] and the Attorney General will invalidate all visas issued to Iranian citizens for future entry into the United States, effective today. We will not reissue visas, nor will we issue new visas, except for compelling and proven humanitarian reasons or where the national interest of our own country requires. This directive will be interpreted very strictly."

Picture of an anti-Iran demonstration in Washington, D.C.

Unfortunately, Carter's efforts would accomplish little in terms of the crisis. There were a number of reasons for this, but the most prominent one was the nature of those men holding the hostages. They were extremists, convinced that what they were doing was not for any political or financial gain but for the glory of God. Also, like most religious zealots, they valued and even longed for martyrdom, so they were not concerned about American retaliation. In the same vein, they were uninterested in money or the kinds of assets that could be sanctioned. As for Iranians in America to visit family or study, they were widely considered traitors anyway.

Thus, as the measures were implemented, the hostages remained where they were.

Chapter 4: Eagle Claw

"The rescue plan—code-named Eagle Claw was not simple. Using eight helicopters, an assault force of 118 men would make their way from the carrier Nimitz in the Gulf of Oman to a desert location in Iran—Desert One. There, they would refuel their huge RH-53D Sea Stallion helicopters from C-130 fuel-carrying planes. Then, through a several-step process, aided by operatives already in place in Tehran, the team would stealthily make their way to the U.S. embassy. Through human intelligence capacities the exact location of the hostages in the embassy was known. The Delta Force commandos would enter the embassy compound, kill every armed guard they encountered—two head shots each—extract the hostages, and return the hostages home safely. Everybody understood that each phase of the operation entailed risks and nobody thought it would be easy. Task Force Commander General James Vaught personally briefed President Carter on the overall operation just a few days before it was to be launched. Carter listened with his usual intensity. Delta Force commander Colonel Beckwith then specifically explained to the president how his people would rescue the hostages. … As the meeting came to a close, President Carter asked to speak privately with Colonel Beckwith. The president said, 'I want you, before you leave for Iran, to assemble all your force and when you think it's appropriate give them a message from me. Tell them that in the event this operation fails, for whatever reason, the fault will not be theirs, it will be mine.'" – David Farber, *Taken Hostage: The Iran Hostage Crisis and America's First Encounter with Radical Islam* (2005)

By the end of April 1980, Carter knew that his political future hung on his ability to see the Iran hostages rescued. Less than six months away from his bid for reelection, he was considered by many Americans to be ineffectual and incompetent, not just due to foreign policy but also the increasingly worsening economy. Just months before the Iran hostage crisis had begun, he had delivered the "malaise" speech, now notoriously remembered as one of the touchstones of his presidency.

With things remaining at an impasse, Carter decided to attempt a rescue operation by sending a group of commandos in to get the Americans out of Iran. According to Eric Haney, a sergeant with Delta Force, "The plan was for the air force to fly us on C-130 aircraft into Desert One, a site about 250 miles from Tehran, where we would meet helicopters coming from the USS Nimitz in the Indian Ocean. The 130s carried big rubber bladders holding thousands of gallons of fuel. We would refuel the helicopters, then move forward that same night to Desert Two, a hide site about forty miles outside the city. The planes would then return to Masirah, off the coast of Oman. That night we would scale the embassy walls—we'd assault the buildings, kill the hostage-holders, and recover the hostages. The hostages would be loaded and immediately carried out, and we would follow."

Pictures from the USS *Nimitz* of Americans preparing for the mission

In detailing his decision before Congress, Carter later explained, "On April 24, 1980, elements of the United States Armed Forces under my direction commenced the positioning stage of a rescue operation which was designed…to effect the rescue of the American hostages who have been held captive in Iran since November 4, 1979…. The subsequent phases of the operation were not executed. Instead…all these elements were withdrawn from Iran and no hostilities occurred. The sole objective of the operation that actually occurred was to position the rescue team for the subsequent effort to withdraw the American hostages. The rescue team was under my overall command and control and required my approval before executing the subsequent phases of the operation designed to effect the rescue itself. No such approval was requested or given because…the mission was aborted."

In other words, not only was the mission a failure, it was aborted before it ever truly began. With those words still ringing in his listeners' ears, Carter continued, "Beginning approximately 10:30 AM EST on April 24, six U.S. C-130 transport aircraft and eight RH-53 helicopters entered Iran airspace. Their crews were not equipped for combat. Some of the C-130 aircraft carried a force of approximately 90 members of the rescue team equipped for combat, plus various support personnel. From approximately 2 to 4 PM EST the six transports and six of the eight helicopters landed at a remote desert site in Iran approximately 200 miles from Tehran where they disembarked the rescue team, commenced refueling operations and began to prepare for the subsequent phases. During the flight to the remote desert site, two of the eight helicopters developed operating difficulties. One was forced to return to the carrier Nimitz; the second was forced to land in the desert, but its crew was taken aboard another of the helicopters and proceeded on to the landing site. Of the six helicopters which landed at the remote desert site, one developed .a serious hydraulic problem and was unable to continue with the mission. The operational plans called for a minimum of six helicopters in good operational condition able to proceed from the desert site. Eight helicopters had been included in the force to provide sufficient redundancy without imposing excessive strains on the refueling and exit requirements of the operation. When the number of helicopters available to continue dropped to five, it was determined that the operation could not proceed as planned. Therefore, on the recommendation of the force commander and my military advisers, I decided to cancel the mission and ordered the United States Armed Forces involved to return from Iran."

John Carney, an Air Force combat controller with Delta Force, explained what went wrong: "The problem was the helicopter part, the Marine pilots. They hadn't been trained in this type of mission. We needed guys with experience landing in the dirt, like in Vietnam. When you try to land one of those big helicopters in the dirt, it just browns out. You can't see anything. ... They'd launched eight helicopters from the Nimitz. The one major contingency of the mission was that we had to have six. That was the absolute minimum. Six helicopters made it to Desert One. Now you're high-fiving: 'We did it—let's go!' And then it just turned to manure. One of the helicopters shut down; his backup hydraulic system was out. That left us with five helicopters—an automatic abort. We'd kept the engines running the whole time, and one of the airplanes was running low on fuel. Its pilot needed to get out of there so he'd have enough fuel to get back to Masirah. The decision was made to move the helicopters out from behind the aircraft [to clear the runway]. One helicopter picked up to reposition and browned out. This is a ninety-mile-per-hour wash coming down into the sand and then blowing it up; he can't see anything."

Due to the lack of visibility and the lack of experience, one of the helicopters went down, with fatal consequences. J. J. Beyers, an Air Force radio operator, recalled, "All of a sudden, the whole windscreen of the airplane lit up. I made it from the cockpit to the door; the whole airplane was on fire. Two shadows on the ground grabbed me and threw me on the ground. That was the last thing I remember. Evidently, I was on fire." Looking back, Haney saw what had gone wrong and reported, "The blades cut through the fuselage and the flight deck, and that pulled the helicopter up on top of the plane—that's when the helicopter exploded." Carney concluded, "It killed three Marines in the back of the helicopter and five airmen who were trapped in the cockpit of the plane."

Pictures of the wreckage

Had the mission simply been aborted and the men returned safely home, it still would have been a failure and a black mark against Carter's presidency, but the deadly circumstances surrounding the mission made it a complete disaster that permanently damaged Carter's reelection prospects. Carter told Congress, "During the process of withdrawal, one of the helicopters accidentally collided with one of the C-130 aircraft, which was preparing to take off, resulting in the death of eight personnel and the injury of several others. At this point, the decision was made to load all surviving personnel aboard the remaining C-130 aircraft and to abandon the remaining helicopters at the landing site. Altogether, the United States Armed Forces remained on the ground for a total of approximately three hours. The five remaining aircraft took off about 5:45 PM EST and departed from Iran airspace without further incident at about 8:00 PM EST on April 24. No United States Armed Forces remain in Iran. The remote desert area was selected to conceal this phase of the mission from discovery. At no time during the temporary presence of United States Armed Forces in Iran did they encounter Iranian forces of any type. We believe, in fact, that no Iranian military forces were in the desert area, and that the Iranian forces were unaware of the presence of United States Armed Forces until after their departure from Iran. As planned, no hostilities occurred during this phase of the mission-the only phase that was executed."

With eight American soldiers dead and the hostages in more danger than they had been before, Carter could only try to mask the failure by drawing attention to the heroism of the men who died: "Our rescue team knew, and I knew, that the operation was certain to be dangerous. We were all convinced that if and when the rescue phase of the operation had been commenced, it had an excellent chance of success. They were all volunteers; they were all highly trained. I met with their leaders before they went on this operation. They knew then what hopes of mine and of all Americans they carried with them. I share with the nation the highest respect and appreciation for the ability and bravery of all who participated in the mission. To the families of those who died and who were injured, I have expressed the admiration I feel for the courage of their loved ones and the sorrow that I feel personally for their sacrifice. The mission on which they were embarked was a humanitarian mission. It was not directed against Iran. It was not directed against the people of Iran. It caused no Iranian casualties."

If his explanation to Congress was difficult, breaking the news to the American people about what had happened was a nightmare. In trying to explain the mission and its objectives, he was forced to admit, "Late yesterday, I cancelled a carefully planned operation which was underway in Iran to position our rescue team for later withdrawal of American hostages, who have been held captive there since November 4. Equipment failure in the rescue helicopters made it necessary to end the mission. As our team was withdrawing, after my order to do so, two of our American aircraft collided on the ground following a refueling operation in a remote desert location in Iran. Other information about this rescue mission will be made available to the American people when it is appropriate to do so. There was no fighting; there was no combat. But to my deep regret, eight of the crewmen of the two aircraft which collided were killed, and several other Americans were hurt in the accident. Our people were immediately airlifted from Iran. Those who were injured have gotten medical treatment, and all of them are expected to recover. No knowledge of this operation by any Iranian officials or authorities was evident to us until several hours after all Americans were withdrawn from Iran."

Well aware that the public was tired of the ongoing crisis and exasperated with the excuses about why so few concrete actions were being taken, Carter continued, "Planning for this rescue effort began shortly after our Embassy was seized, but for a number of reasons, I waited until now to put those rescue plans into effect. To be feasible, this complex operation had to be the product of intensive planning and intensive training and repeated rehearsal. However, a resolution of this crisis through negotiations and with voluntary action on the part of the Iranian officials was obviously then, has been, and will be preferable. This rescue attempt had to await my judgment that the Iranian authorities could not or would not resolve this crisis on their own initiative. With the steady unraveling of authority in Iran and the mounting dangers that were posed to the safety of the hostages themselves and the growing realization that their early release was highly unlikely, I made a decision to commence the rescue operations plans. This attempt became a necessity and a duty. The readiness of our team to undertake the rescue made it completely practicable. Accordingly, I made the decision to set our long-developed plans into operation. I ordered this rescue mission prepared in order to safeguard American lives, to protect America's national interests, and to reduce the tensions in the world that have been caused among many nations as this crisis has continued."

In concluding his remarks, Carter admitted, "It was my decision to attempt the rescue operation. It was my decision to cancel it when problems developed in the placement of our rescue team for a future rescue operation. The responsibility is fully my own."

Just as importantly, the disastrous mission ensured no similar plan would be carried out. As Haney put it, "There's an old army maxim: 'No plan survives contact with the enemy.' We didn't even have to contact the enemy on that one. No plan survives contact with yourself sometimes. When we got home, we started preparations for a second go-round, but it was obvious that no one from the White House had their heart in it. The hostage-takers were worried about the possibility of another attempt, so they scattered the Americans around Iran. It was our one opportunity, and it was gone."

Chapter 5: The Hostage Crisis Dragged Out

"Throughout the election campaign the hostage crisis dragged on. The Carter administration, in the weeks and then months after the failed rescue operation, tried—at last—to draw attention away from the hostages' plight and the government's inability to get them home. Though Carter continued working hard to resolve the crisis, publicly, he drew away from the seemingly endless debacle. But CBS News anchor Walter Cronkite kept counting out the days of the hostages' captivity and ABC continued to remind the American people of the hostages' plight on its nightly news program, rechristened Nightline. While host Ted Koppel occasionally featured other breaking news stories, the focus remained on Iran. With dirty yellow ribbons hanging everywhere in the United States, the American people had grown numb to the ordeal—if no more satisfied with Carter's failure to bring the hostages home. ... That July the Iranian hostage-takers had shown a bit of humanity by releasing another hostage who was suffering from multiple sclerosis. But for the other fifty-two Americans still in Iran, scattered around the country, the months went by in dull misery. Iran remained mired in instability. In June fierce armed clashes broke out between leftists and Islamic fundamentalists. Political divisions within the Iranian military upped the anxiety level throughout Iranian society. Control of the revolution was by no means finalized." – David Farber, *Taken Hostage: The Iran Hostage Crisis and America's First Encounter with Radical Islam* (2005)

Joseph Hall, who had been a military attaché at the embassy when it was captured, recalled that in the days following the failed rescue attempt the captors "panicked and spread us all over the country in forty-eight hours. I think I was moved seventeen times during the next two months." From that time until their release, the hostages were in a heightened state of anxiety, as each day brought more news or, worse, none at all. Marine Rocky Sickmann recalled, "One day the guards brought over a copy of *The Sporting News*, and I'm sitting there reading that a tennis tournament was postponed 'due to the death of the Shah of Iran.' I said, 'Holy shit!' We bang on the door: 'Hey, Ali'—everybody's name was Ali; they wouldn't give us their real names—'What is this, the frickin' Shah is dead?'"

Indeed, the Shah did die in Egypt on July 27, 1980, adding more uncertainty to the equation. Abolhassan Banisadr, who would subsequently become president of Iran, remembered, "The consequences of the rescue mission were severe. The mullahs' suspicions were raised against the military, because they wondered how the U.S. could enter Iranian airspace undetected. So they started a purge that resulted in the extreme weakening of Iran's military power. ... [The Shah's] passing wasn't something the students were happy about. As long as the Shah was alive, they could use the excuse that he was planning to come back, that he was a direct threat to the government."

Banisadr (with glasses) during the hostage crisis

According to hostage John Limbert, "His death didn't affect the way we were treated. It was clear this whole incident was not about the United States—it was an internal political game. One of the students even said that to me. They had been turned into prison guards. I think many of them felt used by the politicians."

By the summer of 1980, the hostages themselves were beginning to run out of patience. Ode wrote in August, "The student who took me out for sun today asked me if I was learning any Iranian (Persian). I told him since I never intended to return to Iran once I am set free, I have no use for or intention of learning any Farsi. I told him that I once had some Iranian friends in Switzerland but no longer intended to associate with any Iranians. He asked me if they were better than the students here. I told him that they seemed like nice people at the time and at least when I was invited to their homes they let me go home when I wished, which was not the case here. He said that 'Life is a school' and that I 'shouldn't worry' (which is their usual response to everything: 'Don't worry about it, it isn't important!') I told him that if life is a school, this is a bit of learning I could do without and that the only thing I had learned was to hate Iran and all Iranians and that I would hate this country and everyone connected with it for the rest of my life!"

By this point, Ode and the others were becoming increasingly aware that as bad as the situation was for them, the situation for their captors was not much better. Moorhead Kennedy, an economics and commercial officer, observed, "[O]nce, when they were moving us, one of the guards stood there with tears pouring down his cheeks. He was a local hire, and when we were moved he was laid off. This was obviously the most exciting moment of his life; terrorism gives a lot of unemployed people something exciting to do." Ode himself recorded a particularly insightful observation when he wrote on August 6, "Akbar still isn't back from wherever he is. I believe he is on one of the summer farm work projects that the students participate in to show their affinity for the "downtrodden" which, of course, is a lot of BS. Anyway, when he isn't here, nothing seems to run really right. Mohammed still hasn't given us any of the mail that was supposed to have arrived two days ago and he isn't here either or at least isn't paying any attention to us. I'll be glad when Ramadan is over, which it should be on either August 10 or 11 (was told Ramadan lasts for 29 days and it began on July 13, so hopefully August 10 is the last day). Perhaps then things will begin to show some semblance of order again. I think most of the students stay up all night celebrating Ramadan and doing their eating, and then sleep all day."

Mansour Farhang, the first Iranian ambassador to the United Nations since the revolution, would later confirm that over time, the hostage takers developed a sense of having been betrayed themselves: "The hostage-taking probably cost Iran over $10 billion. Khomeini didn't care; he enjoyed his immense popularity and the idea of being involved in a moral struggle. The sanctions, the freezing of Iran's assets, were devastating. Without the economic weakness and international isolation, Saddam Hussein would not have invaded Iran in September 1980. There was hardly any resistance."

In writing about conditions following Hussein's September 22 invasion, Ode noted, "Shortly thereafter old Hamid came in 'just to see how we were' (so he said). I asked him what the 'war' was all about and how did they feel knowing they had enemies? He said that it was only 'for practice' which, of course I don't believe since they have been much too scared the past few months for it to be just 'practice' which they would have been aware of. Just whose planes they were shooting at, of course, I don't know. It would be good to know that they are ours--and I would even be glad if they were Russian. It might make these jerks realize that they are opposing powerful forces and it is high time to learn that they are playing with fire to keep opposing the U.S. with Russia right on their border."

Ode went on to record how he castigated his captors for the poor treatment he was receiving: "I harped at him about how their entire system was wrong; how the students (whom I called terrorists) went out of their way to make us angry and then wondered why we became so. I told him that they were exceptionally cruel and unkind which he denied, saying that they were not 'terrorists' but students but I told him that when I am kept for almost a year in a locked room, constantly guarded by so-called 'students' with loaded guns, when I couldn't even go to the toilet or for showers without being blindfolded and constantly guarded--then, in my opinion, they were terrorists and had no right to call themselves anything else. I reminded him about how cruel they were to my wife to keep us separated, especially since I was no longer a young man, had never had anything to do with Iran before I came here, that I was sent here for 45 days and have been held for almost a year and am treated like a child, and that when they do things like this they are 'terrorists' pure and simple and had long ago ceased to be students. He said that they tried to be kind to us but that 'our government' was the one that was difficult as it wouldn't agree to anything. I reminded him again that I told him and other student-terrorists right from the first day of our captivity that the U.S. Government would never agree to negotiate with 'gangsters and terrorists' and that while they may not consider themselves to be terrorists and gangsters, that is exactly what they are regarded in the eyes of the world."

Chapter 6: Trying to Finalize the Deal

"Poor Jimmy Carter had worked tirelessly, as was his wont, in the last days of his presidency trying to finalize the deal that would free the hostages. ...he literally camped out in the Oval Office, waiting to hear that the hostages would be freed while he was still president. ... Not until the next day, five minutes after Carter turned over the presidency to Ronald Reagan, were the hostages freed by their Iranian captors. Reagan sent Carter and the core group of men who had worked for so long on the hostage crisis to Germany, where the ex-hostages flew after their brief stop in Algeria. It was an emotional meeting. Some of the hostages had hard questions for the former president, asking why he had allowed the Shah into the United States despite warnings from the embassy and why he had attempted a military rescue that could have endangered their lives. ... On the way home, Carter turned to Hamilton Jordan, the man who had been with him since he had started his presidential odyssey, and said: 'You know, Ham, if we had had a little luck back in March or April and gotten 'em out then, we might be flying back to Washington instead of Plains.' Probably not, given all the other troubles too many Americans blamed on Carter's presidency, but who can say for sure?" – David Farber, *Taken Hostage: The Iran Hostage Crisis and America's First Encounter with Radical Islam* (2005)

In mid-September 1980, Khomeini released a new set of demands in exchange for the hostages' release. The ayatollah insisted that the Shah's wealth be returned to the people of Iran (and thus his control), and that Iranian assets then being held in America be unfrozen. For the most part, this was a form of last minute bluster, because Khomeini knew that he might have a major problem looming on the horizon. Presidential candidate Ronald Reagan had run much of his campaign criticizing Carter's handling of the crisis, and during the last debate, he stated, "I have been accused lately of having a secret plan with regard to the hostages. Now, this comes from an answer that I've made at least 50 times during this campaign to the press. The question would be, 'Have you any ideas of what you would do if you were there?' And I said, well, yes. ... These are just ideas of what I would think of if I were in that position and had access to the information, in which I would know all the options that were open to me. I have never answered the question, however. Second — the one that says, 'Well, tell me, what are some of those ideas?' First of all, I would be fearful that I might say something that was presently under way or in negotiations, and thus expose it and endanger the hostages. And sometimes, I think some of my ideas might involve quiet diplomacy, where you don't say in advance or say to anyone what it is you're thinking of doing. … What I do think should be done, once they are safely here with their families and that tragedy is over — and we've endured this humiliation for just lacking 1 week of a year now — then, I think, it is time for us to have a complete investigation as to the diplomatic efforts that were made in the beginning, why they have been there so long, and when they come home, what did we have to do in order to bring that about, what arrangements were made?"

Reagan

In fact, unbeknownst to most Americans, Reagan had already been working behind the scenes to try to get the hostages freed. Banisadr explained, "In the spring of 1980, the Reagan-and-Bush team contacted my team and also the Islamic Republican Party, the friends of Mr. Khomeini. Reagan's team tried to make a deal with us to free the hostages. I rejected the deal because they weren't official representatives of the U.S. at the time, but the Islamic Republican Party decided to work with them. [As a result] Khomeini delayed implementation of the release until Reagan was elected."

Reagan also emphasized that there would be dire consequences if the hostages were not freed by the time he came into office. Reagan campaign advisor David Gergen recalled, "In the U.S., election day 1980 fell on the one-year anniversary of the hostage-taking. It was clearly a factor in Reagan's ten-point defeat of Carter. I am among those who believe the coming to office of Reagan was a significant factor in the Iranians' decision to free the hostages. I remember one common quip going around was: What's flat, red, and glows in the dark? Answer: Tehran, after Reagan becomes president."

Back in Iran, the hostages were pinning their hopes on the idea that a new president could get them out of Iran. Hall noted, "We didn't know if it meant anything or not, but we were counting down to inauguration day. On January 19, they led me into a room and asked me questions about my treatment. I remember they presented it as though I was a 'candidate for release.' I wasn't going to sing their praises, but I wasn't going to say a whole lot." Limbert was also questioned, during which he told his captors, "You could have done a good thing with your revolution, but you really screwed it up."

Even after he was defeated in November 1980, Carter worked tirelessly to bring the remaining hostages home, and he finally struck a deal in the eleventh hour for their release. On January 19, just days before handing over the presidency to Reagan, Carter was able to announce, "We have now reached an agreement with Iran which will result, I believe, in the freedom of our American hostages. The last documents have now been signed in Algiers, following the signing of the documents in Iran which will result in this agreement. We still have a few documents to sign before the money is actually transferred and the hostages are released. The essence of the agreement is that following the release of our hostages, then we will unfreeze and transfer to the Iranians a major part of the assets which were frozen by me when the Iranians seized our Embassy compound and took our hostages. We have also reached complete agreement on the arbitration procedures between ourselves and Iran with the help of the Algerians which will resolve the claims that exist between residents of our Nation and Iran and vice-versa. ... We don't yet know exactly how fast this procedure will go. We are prepared to move as rapidly as possible. All the preparations have been completed pending the final documents being signed."

Back in Iran, the hostages learned that the big day had finally come. Sickmann recalled, "On January 20, they told us we were going home. They came back five minutes later and we were still sitting there. Seriously. You have to understand that they have screwed with our minds for

444 days. I remember walking out that night. They had taken our shoes away, and we had plastic sandals. I was blindfolded, and it was snowing; the snow was running through my toes as I was walking through it. I can hear to this day the crunching of the snow under my feet as we walked to this bus that supposedly was taking us to the airport. … We walk to the back of the airplane. Nobody high-fives, nobody says a word. You're free, but you're still whispering to each other because you're in shock. The plane starts revving and shaking, and all of a sudden it comes to an idle. It's like, 'God, they're messing with us.' Iran had turned off the runway lights."

Ted Koppel, whose television news show *Nightline* had been built around monitoring the hostage crisis, described what happened: "The hostages were on the plane, but the Iranians did the cruelest thing they could think of, which was to wait until one second after noon on inauguration day. And that was just crushing. Carter and Brzezinski and their advisers were in the Oval Office all night, praying that they would get these guys released while they were still on duty. Because Carter really did, it must be said, try with all his heart to get those men and women out of there." Bill Daugherty, with the CIA, tried to explain the Iranians' motives: "You cannot underestimate the hatred that the hostage-takers felt for Jimmy Carter. They felt betrayed by him. He had come in on a platform of human rights, and he had said these standards will apply to friends as well as enemies. He mentioned Iran in the campaign! The Iranians really believed he was going to come in and stop the Shah's human-rights violations."

Many of those waiting for the hostages' arrival were concerned that once the plane was in the air, militant Iranians might shoot it down. Warren Christopher, Carter's Secretary of State, later conceded, "The Iranians sent two commercial planes, one as a decoy. But until I saw the landing lights of those planes off in the distance, near the Algiers airport, I had no real confidence that they were coming home. It was a very tricky moment."

It would be impossible for anyone who had not been in their situation to appreciate the hostages' feelings when they finally reached freedom. Sickmann remembered, "We got off the airplane in Algiers and kissed the ground. The left cheek of my pants was completely ripped out from sitting on my can so much. I felt sorry for the ambassador and all the other people having to look at us and smell us." According to hostage Michael Metrinko, "When we got to the military hospital at Wiesbaden [in Germany], there were stacks of newspapers in the reception area. I was glancing at one, and I looked at one of the photographs and thought, My God, it looks just like my grandfather's portrait. Then I realized it was the portrait that hung in our dining room at home, and that the people standing under it were my mother and father. Why it would be in The New York Times I had no idea. I did not know that anyone was interested or cared. It was like Rip Van Winkle waking up."

Pictures of the former hostages at the hospital

To his credit, Reagan graciously allowed Carter to represent the United States in meeting with the hostages in Algiers. This proved to be something of a mixed blessing for the former president since many of hostages blamed Carter for their capture and confinement, and some even refused to meet with the now former president. Al Golacinski noted that there were some tense moments during the meeting: "A gentleman stood up—I will not reveal who he was—and said to the president, 'Why did you do the one thing that would fire up the Iranians like that?' His answer was, 'We had been given assurances that our embassy and our personnel would be protected.' I stood up and said, 'Mr. President, with all due respect, I and others wrote that those assurances were not worth the paper they were written on.' Later we had our pictures taken individually with the president, and he apologized to me. He said he had seen what had been written. I really believe the president was a very decent man."

The freed hostages finally came home on January 25, 1981, but nearly 35 years later, the embassy in Teheran remains closed and formal diplomatic relations between the United States and Iran having not been reestablished. The Great Seal of the United States, damaged and defaced, remains over the entrance, as if waiting to greet – and warn - a future ambassador to the country.

Online Resources

Other titles about 20th century history by Charles River Editors

Other titles about the Iran hostage crisis on Amazon

Bibliography

Bakhash, Shaul (1984). The Reign of the Ayatollahs: Iran and the Islamic Revolution. Basic Books.

Bowden, Mark (2006). Guests of the Ayatollah: The Iran Hostage Crisis: The First Battle in America's War with Militant Islam. New York: Grove Press. ISBN 0-87113-925-1

Ebtekar, Massoumeh; Reed, Fred (2000). Takeover in Tehran: The Inside Story of the 1979 U.S. Embassy Capture. Burnaby, BC: Talonbooks. ISBN 0-88922-443-9

Harris, Les (1997). 444 Days to Freedom: What Really Happened in Iran. DVD UPC 033909253390

Moin, Baqer (2000). Khomeini: Life of the Ayatollah. Thomas Dunne Books.

Sick, Gary (1991). October Surprise: America's Hostages in Iran and the Election of Ronald Reagan. New York: Random House.

Made in the USA
Middletown, DE
09 December 2018